This book b

_ _

Rose Tincture

Ingredients:

Fresh rose petals (organic and pesticide-free)

High-proof alcohol (such as vodka or brandy)

Instructions

Begin by gathering fresh rose petals from organic and pesticide-free sources. It's best to pick the petals on a dry day, preferably in the morning when the flowers are at their peak.

Thoroughly wash the rose petals under cold water to remove any dirt, debris, or bugs. Dry gently.

In a clean glass jar with a tight-fitting lid, place the washed rose petals. Ensure that the jar is large enough to accommodate both the rose petals and the alcohol.

Pour the high-proof alcohol over the rose petals in the jar, making sure they are fully submerged. Use enough alcohol to cover the petals completely.

Seal the jar tightly with the lid and give it a gentle shake to ensure that the rose petals are evenly distributed and fully immersed in the alcohol.

Place the jar in a cool, dark place to steep for at least 4-6 weeks. The longer you let the mixture steep, the stronger the tincture will be. Some people prefer to steep their tincture for up to 8 weeks for maximum potency.

Shake the jar gently every few days to help release the active compounds from the rose petals and ensure thorough extraction. After the steeping period is complete, strain the tincture through a fine mesh sieve, cheesecloth, or coffee filter into a clean glass bottle or dropper bottle. Squeeze or press the rose petals to extract any liquid.

Store the rose tincture in a cool, dark place away from direct sunlight. Properly stored, it should remain potent for several months to a year.

Label the bottle with the contents and date of preparation for easy identification.

In gardens fair,
where petals bloom,

Where morning
dew adorns each
room,

There dwells a
flower, both sweet
and wise,

With velvety hues
that
mesmerize.

Oh, rose divine, with
petals rare,

In whispered secrets,
you declare

The mysteries of love's
embrace,

In every delicate,
blushing trace.

Your fragrance, like
a whispered sigh,

Through windswept
fields, it gently flies,

And in your essence,
we find repose,

Amidst life's thorns,
where beauty grows.

In crimson robes, you
stand so tall,

A symbol of love,
surpassing all,

For in their
presence, we find our
muse,

In every petal,
love infused.

With every bloom, a
tale untold,

In your embrace,
hearts unfold.

Cranberry Rose Jelly

Ingredients:

3 cups cranberry juice

1 cup water

1 cup granulated sugar

1 tablespoon rose water or rose oil (food-grade)

1 packet (about 1.75 ounces) powdered pectin

Instructions

In a medium saucepan, combine the cranberry juice and water. Bring the mixture to a gentle boil over medium heat.

Once boiling, reduce the heat to low and let the mixture simmer for about 10-15 minutes to reduce slightly.

In a small bowl, mix the powdered pectin with a small amount of sugar to prevent clumping.

Add the pectin-sugar mixture to the simmering cranberry juice, stirring continuously to prevent lumps from forming.

Add the remaining granulated sugar and rose water or rose oil to the saucepan, stirring until the sugar has completely dissolved.

Continue to simmer the mixture over low heat for an additional 10-15 minutes, stirring occasionally, until it thickens to a jelly-like consistency.

Remove the saucepan from the heat and let the cranberry jelly cool slightly.

Pour the cranberry jelly into sterilized jars or molds. Optionally, garnish with rose petals.

Allow the cranberry jelly to cool to room temperature before transferring it to the refrigerator to set completely. Let it chill in the refrigerator for at least 4 hours, or overnight, until fully set.

Once set, the cranberry jelly is ready to serve! Enjoy it on toast, with cheese, or as a sweet addition to your favorite dishes.

Journal

A Year of Roses

A Verity Rose Romance

Title: A Year of Roses

Chapter 1: The Whispers of Roses

In the picturesque town of Willow Creek, nestled amidst rolling hills and winding streams, a quaint flower shop stood that captured the essence of romance. The shop, adorned with ivy-covered walls and bursts of colorful blooms, was a haven for lovers and dreamers alike.

Arabella's flower shop was more than just a place of business—it was a haven of love and tranquility, where the air was always filled with the scent of roses and the promise of romance lingered in every corner. The entrance, a cobblestone courtyard adorned with quaint wrought-iron benches, invited visitors to linger and lose themselves in the magic of the moment.

Within the courtyard, the gentle murmur of water flowing from fountains mingled with the melodic chirping of birds, creating a symphony of sounds that soothed the soul and stirred the heart. Here, amidst the timeless beauty of nature, one could lose oneself in the embrace of serenity and find solace in the simple pleasures of life.

Arabella, the owner of the flower shop, possessed a rare beauty that seemed to transcend time. With her sparkling green eyes and a smile that could melt even the coldest of hearts, she was the epitome of grace and elegance.

Arabella's days at the flower shop were a delicate dance of beauty and grace, each moment infused with the subtle fragrance of blooms and the gentle rustle of petals.

From the time she stepped through the door each morning, Arabella greeted each customer with a warm smile and a genuine enthusiasm for the beauty that surrounded them. With an expert eye and a tender touch, she carefully curated bouquets and arrangements, selecting the perfect combination of flowers to convey the sentiment of each occasion.

In between serving customers and tending to the shop's needs, Arabella found moments of quiet reflection amidst the blooms. She would pause to inhale the sweet fragrance of roses, letting their perfume transport her to a world of beauty and possibility.

As each day drew to a close and the shop grew quiet, Arabella would take one last lingering look around, a sense of fulfillment warming her heart. For in the world of flowers, she had found not just a business, but a calling—a passion that filled her days with joy and purpose, and infused every interaction with the timeless beauty of nature's bounty.

Chapter 2: Seasons of Roses

As the seasons changed and the world around them transformed, Arabella's flower shop remained a beacon of constancy amidst the ebb and flow of time. While other flowers came and went with the passing of the seasons, the roses remained a steadfast presence, their velvety petals a symbol of enduring love and timeless romance.

In the courtyard, the roses bloomed in a kaleidoscope of colors, their delicate fragrance filling the air with a heady perfume that intoxicated the senses and stirred the soul. Here, amidst the beauty of nature's bounty, one could find solace in the simple elegance of a single rose and lose themselves in the splendor of the moment.

It started on the first Monday in June. As Arabella stepped through the courtyard, she could feel something was different. There was a strange energy in the air.

As she approached her shop, her heart quickened at the sight of a solitary rose, its petals adorned in the most magnificent shade of coral pink, nestled gently on the doorstep. With trembling hands, she reached for the delicate bloom, its velvety touch sending a shiver of anticipation down her spine. And there, nestled beside the rose, was a note—a simple yet profound declaration that spoke volumes in its brevity: "A rose for a rose."

As Arabella's fingers brushed against the velvety petals of the exquisite bloom, a surge of recognition washed over her. It was no ordinary rose that graced her doorstep—it was the legendary Sweet Juliet rose, renowned as the world's most coveted and expensive flower.

Its delicate fragrance filled the air, intoxicating her senses with its ethereal perfume, as if whispering secrets of mystery. At that moment, as she cradled the precious bloom in her hands, Arabella felt a flutter in her heart—a sense of wonder and awe.

Every Monday morning, like clockwork, a rare pink rose would appear at the doorstep of the flower shop, nestled among the other blossoms. Arabella would marvel at its exquisite beauty, the delicate petals unfurling to reveal a hue so ethereal that it seemed to defy reality.

Accompanying the rose was always a handwritten note addressed to her, signed by a mysterious stranger. The words were simple yet filled with intrigue, hinting at a secret admirer who watched her from afar. Arabella couldn't help but feel a flutter of excitement every time she read the note, wondering who this enigmatic individual could be. The words were always the same, "A Rose for a Rose".

Chapter 3: The Mystery Continues

As the weeks passed, the mystery of the rose deepened, leaving Arabella both intrigued and perplexed. Who was the mysterious stranger who left her these tokens of affection? And what did they hope to achieve by sending them?

Determined to unravel the mystery, Arabella began to pay closer attention to her surroundings, searching for any clues that might lead her to the identity of her secret admirer. She would linger by the window of her flower shop, casting furtive glances at the passersby, hoping to catch a glimpse of the one who held her heart in their hands.

Meanwhile, unbeknownst to Arabella, the mysterious stranger watched her from a distance, his admiration growing with each passing day. He was a rose grower by trade, tending to fields of blossoms that paled in comparison to the beauty of the woman he admired from afar.

Chapter 4: Nathaniel

Once a month, Arabella's heart would quicken its pace in anticipation of Nathaniel's arrival. He was her supplier. Like clockwork, he would appear at her shop promptly at 2:00, his presence casting a spell over her that she couldn't quite shake. Arabella found herself drawn to him in a way she couldn't explain.

With each passing meeting, she dared to hope that Nathaniel would ask her out to lunch, to spend more time together beyond the confines of business. And so, she took extra care in her preparations, adorning herself in a new dress that accentuated her curves, her hair styled to perfection, and her makeup applied with an artist's touch.

As she awaited Nathaniel's arrival, her heart fluttered with a mixture of excitement and longing, her mind filled with dreams of what could be. And as the clock ticked closer to 2:00, she couldn't help but wonder if today would be the day. Did he know? Could he feel the pull as well?

Nathaniel was a man shrouded in an enigmatic allure, his presence commanding attention wherever he went. Tall and imposing, he carried himself with a quiet confidence that spoke of a depth of character beyond his years. His dark hair framed a face chiseled with strong, angular features, his piercing gaze holding a hint of mystery that drew others in like moths to a flame.

There was an air of elegance about Nathaniel, a refinement that set him apart from the crowd. His manner was reserved yet captivating, his words carefully chosen as if each one held a hidden meaning waiting to be unraveled. And though he spoke little, his silence held a power all its own, leaving those around him hanging on his every word.

But it was not just Nathaniel's appearance that captivated Arabella—it was the aura of mystery that surrounded him like a cloak, beckoning her to delve deeper into the secrets he kept hidden beneath the surface. And as she gazed into his dark, inscrutable eyes, Arabella felt herself drawn into a world of intrigue and possibility, where the promise of love and adventure awaited just beyond the horizon.

Chapter 5: The Echo of Unspoken Words

As the meeting drew to a close, Arabella's heart brimmed with anticipation, her longing for answers burning brighter than ever before. With a gentle smile, she thanked Nathaniel for his time, her eyes lingering on him for just a moment longer.

But as Nathaniel rose from his seat, a flicker of uncertainty crossed his features, his gaze darting away as if searching for an escape. Sensing his unease, Arabella took a deep breath, summoning the courage to voice the question that had been weighing on her mind.

"Nathaniel," she began, her voice trembling with emotion, "before you go, there's something I've been meaning to ask you. Tell me about the rare rose, the Sweet Juliet. I've heard whispers of its beauty, but I long to know more."

For a fleeting moment, Nathaniel's expression softened, his eyes betraying a hint of vulnerability that sent a shiver down Arabella's spine. But before he could respond, a sudden urgency seemed to grip him, his demeanor shifting as he glanced at his watch.

"I'm sorry, Arabella," he said, his tone tinged with regret, "but I must go. I have another meeting in the area, and I'm already running late."

With a heavy heart, Arabella watched as Nathaniel hurriedly gathered his belongings, his movements betraying a sense of urgency that left her feeling unsettled. And as he disappeared through the door, leaving her alone with her thoughts, she couldn't shake the feeling that there was more to Nathaniel's abrupt departure than met the eye.

As she sat in the quiet stillness of her shop, the unanswered questions swirling in her mind like a tempest, Arabella couldn't help but wonder what secrets Nathaniel was hiding beneath his stoic facade. And though she knew she may never uncover the truth, she vowed to never stop searching for the answers that lay hidden within the petals of the Sweet Juliet rose.

And that fragrance - where had she encountered that fragrance before?

Chapter 6: The Scent of Intrigue

As Nathaniel bid his farewell and made his hasty exit, leaving Arabella with a longing for answers unfulfilled, she couldn't shake the feeling that something lingered in the air —an elusive scent that teased her senses.

Lost in thought, Arabella found herself drawn to the lingering aroma that danced around her, a faint whisper of a man's cologne that tugged at the edges of her consciousness. It was a scent she had encountered before, though she couldn't quite place where or when.

As the minutes stretched into eternity, Arabella's mind raced with possibilities, her heart yearning for the missing piece of the puzzle that would unlock the secrets hidden within Nathaniel's enigmatic demeanor.

As the last rays of sunlight filtered through the windows of her shop, casting long shadows across the worn wooden floors, Arabella's thoughts were consumed by the bustle of closing time. With a weary smile, she bid farewell to the lingering customers, their laughter and chatter echoing in the empty space as they made their way home.

In the quiet stillness that followed, Arabella found herself enveloped in the familiar routine of tidying up, each task a comforting rhythm that grounded her amidst the chaos of the day.

She carefully arranged any remaining blooms, their vibrant colors fading into the twilight, and dimmed the lights to a soft glow that bathed the shop in a warm embrace.

But even as she went about her duties, a sense of unease lingered in the air—a nagging suspicion that there was more to Nathaniel's sudden departure than met the eye. Try as she might, Arabella couldn't shake the memory of the elusive scent that had haunted her during their meeting, its presence lingering in the corners of her mind like a shadow waiting to be revealed.

And yet, as the hours slipped by and the night descended upon Willow Creek, the demands of her shop pressed upon her like a weight upon her shoulders, pushing thoughts of Nathaniel and his mysterious cologne to the back of her mind. For now, there were tasks to be done, and she couldn't afford to let distractions cloud her focus.

With a final glance around the now-empty shop, Arabella locked the door behind her and stepped out into the cool night air, the faint scent of roses lingering on the breeze. And though the mysteries of the day remained unresolved, she couldn't help but feel a flicker of anticipation stirring within her—a whisper of possibility that hinted at adventures yet to come.

Chapter 7: Echoes of Time

As the weeks turned into months, Arabella found herself caught in the ebb and flow of time, each passing day bringing her closer to the anniversary date of the first rose—the day that had sparked a journey of mystery and longing that had consumed her thoughts and filled her dreams.

In the quiet moments of the night, when the world around her was cloaked in darkness and the stars whispered secrets to the moon, Arabella found solace in the ritual of drying each rose that graced her doorstep. With tender care, she preserved their delicate beauty, placing them in a crystal vase with a lid that shimmered like a jewel in the faint light.

But as the anniversary date loomed on the horizon, Arabella couldn't shake the nagging feeling of uncertainty that gnawed at her heart. The vase, once a symbol of hope and possibility, now stood as a silent reminder of all that remained unanswered—a vessel waiting to be filled with the truth she so desperately sought.

Try as she might, all of Arabella's attempts to uncover the identity of the sender had been in vain. Each lead she pursued, each clue she followed, seemed to slip through her fingers like grains of sand, leaving her grasping at shadows and chasing after ghosts.

And yet, even in the face of uncertainty, Arabella refused to surrender to despair. With each passing day, she clung to the hope that someday, somehow, she would unravel the mystery that had consumed her thoughts and filled her dreams. For deep within her heart, she knew that the journey was far from over—that the echoes of time held secrets yet to be revealed, and that the truth she sought was waiting just beyond the horizon, waiting to be discovered in the fullness of time.

Chapter 8: Whispers of Fate

On the eve of the anniversary of the first rose, as the sun dipped below the horizon and cast its golden glow upon the world, Arabella's heart fluttered with anticipation. She held the note in her trembling hands, the words etched upon the page like a promise waiting to be fulfilled. For the first time in a year, the sender's message was different—a departure from the familiar refrain of "A Rose for a Rose."

As she read the words, inviting her to meet him in the courtyard at half past 8:00, a mixture of excitement and trepidation washed over her. Who was this mysterious sender, and what was the purpose of sending her roses for a year? Amelia's mind raced with questions, her heart pounding in her chest as she dared to hope that the answers she sought were finally within her grasp.

As the appointed hour drew near, Arabella made her way to the courtyard, her pulse quickening with each step. The air was thick with anticipation, the scent of roses mingling with the familiar aroma of a man's cologne—a fragrance that sent shivers of recognition down her spine.

And there, amidst a sea of flickering candles and vases overflowing with the rare Sweet Juliet rose, stood Nathaniel, his eyes alight with a fire that mirrored the longing in Arabella's heart. As she approached him, her breath caught in her throat, her senses overwhelmed by the sheer magnitude of the moment.

With a tender smile, Nathaniel reached for a black box nestled in his palm, his movements deliberate as he lowered himself to one knee. At that moment, time seemed to stand still as he gazed up at her, his eyes shimmering with unspoken emotion.

"Arabella," he whispered, his voice a gentle caress against her skin, "will you marry me?"

And as she looked into his eyes, her heart overflowing with love and joy, Arabella knew that she had found her answer—a resounding "yes" that echoed through the courtyard like a song of hope and possibility. At that moment, surrounded by the beauty of the roses and the warmth of Nathaniel's love, she knew that their journey was only just beginning—a journey filled with endless possibilities and the promise of a future filled with love, laughter, and the sweet fragrance of roses in bloom.

Chapter 9: Echoes of Forever

As the stars twinkled overhead, casting their ethereal glow upon the courtyard, Arabella and Nathaniel exchanged vows of love and commitment beneath the canopy of roses.

Surrounded by the whispered blessings of friends and family, they embarked on a journey together, hand in hand, their hearts intertwined in a bond forged by destiny.
In the years that followed, Arabella and Nathaniel faced their share of trials and tribulations, navigating the winding paths of life with grace and resilience. Through every challenge and triumph, they remained steadfast in their love for one another, their bond growing stronger with each passing day.

And though their story was not without its twists and turns, Arabella and Nathaniel found solace in the knowledge that they were never alone—that together, they could weather any storm, conquer any obstacle, and emerge stronger and more united than ever before.

As they looked back on their journey, Arabella and Nathaniel realized that their love was not just a fairy tale ending, but a testament to the enduring power of love. And as they gazed into each other's eyes, they knew that their love would continue to blossom and grow, casting its radiant light upon the world for all eternity.

Journal

Journal

Journal

Journal

Rose Shortbread Cookies

Ingredients:

1 cup unsalted butter, softened
1/2 cup powdered sugar
2 cups all-purpose flour
1/4 teaspoon salt
1 teaspoon rose water
1 tablespoon dried rose petals
(optional, for garnish)

Instructions

Preheat your oven to 325°F (160°C). Line a baking sheet with parchment paper and set aside.

In a large mixing bowl, cream together the softened butter and powdered sugar until light and fluffy. Gradually add the flour and salt to the butter mixture, mixing until a dough forms. Be careful not to overmix.

Stir in the rose water until well incorporated into the dough. The rose water will give the cookies a subtle floral flavor and aroma.

Roll out the dough on a lightly floured surface to about 1/4 inch thickness. Use a cookie cutter to cut out shapes of your choice. Place the cookies on the prepared baking sheet.

If desired, lightly press dried rose petals onto the tops of the cookies for a decorative touch and an extra hint of rose flavor.

Bake the cookies in the preheated oven for 12-15 minutes, or until the edges are lightly golden brown.

Remove the cookies from the oven and let them cool on the baking sheet for a few minutes before transferring them to a wire rack to cool completely.

Once cooled, serve and enjoy your delicious rose-infused shortbread cookies with a cup of tea or coffee.

These delicate and fragrant cookies are perfect for any occasion!

Journal

Rose Lemonade

Ingredients:

1 cup fresh lemon juice (about
4-6 lemons)
1/2 cup granulated sugar
(adjust to taste)
4 cups cold water
2-3 tablespoons rose water
(adjust to taste)
Ice cubes
Fresh rose petals for garnish

Instructions

In a large pitcher, combine the fresh lemon juice and granulated sugar. Stir well until the sugar is dissolved.
Pour in the cold water and stir to combine.

Start by adding 2 tablespoons of rose water to the pitcher. Taste the lemonade and adjust the amount of rose water to your preference. Add more if you desire a stronger rose flavor.

Stir the lemonade well to evenly distribute the rose water.

Refrigerate the rose lemonade for at least 1 hour to chill and allow the flavors to meld together.

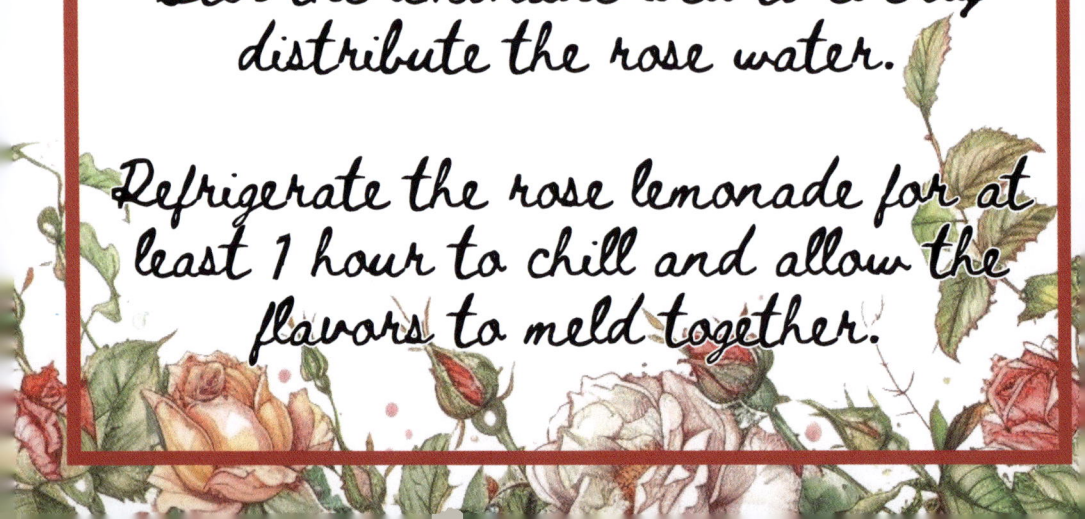

Once chilled, give the lemonade another good stir before serving.

Fill glasses with ice cubes and pour the rose lemonade over the ice.

Garnish each glass with a few fresh rose petals for a beautiful presentation, if desired.

Serve the rose lemonade immediately and enjoy its refreshing and aromatic flavor!

This delightful rose lemonade is perfect for sipping on a hot summer day or for serving on special occasions. Its unique floral aroma and tangy citrus flavor are sure to be a hit with everyone who tries it!

Journal

Rose Water

Ingredients

Fresh rose petals (organic
and pesticide-free)

Distilled water

Instructions

Begin by gathering fresh rose petals. It's best to use organic roses that haven't been treated with pesticides or chemicals.

Rinse the petals gently under cold water to remove any dirt or debris. Place the clean rose petals in a large pot or saucepan. Pour enough distilled water over the petals to just cover them.

Cover the pot with a lid and bring the water to a gentle simmer over low to medium heat.

Allow the petals to simmer for about 30-45 minutes, stirring occasionally. As the water simmers, the rose petals will release their natural oils and fragrance, infusing the water with the essence of roses.

After simmering, remove the pot from the heat and let it cool completely. Once cooled, strain the rose water into a clean glass jar or bottle using a fine mesh strainer or cheesecloth to remove the petals.

Store the homemade rose water in the refrigerator to prolong its freshness. It can be kept for up to 1-2 weeks.

Use the rose water in your favorite recipes, skincare routines, or as a fragrant addition to homemade cosmetics and bath products.

Homemade rose water is a wonderful natural ingredient that adds a delicate floral aroma and flavor to a variety of dishes and beauty products.

Enjoy experimenting with different ways to incorporate it into your daily routine!

Rose Infused Tea

Ingredients:

2 cups water
2 teaspoons dried rose petals (or 4-5 fresh rose petals)
2 teaspoons loose leaf black tea (or tea of your choice)
Honey or sugar (optional, to taste)
Fresh lemon slices (optional, for garnish)

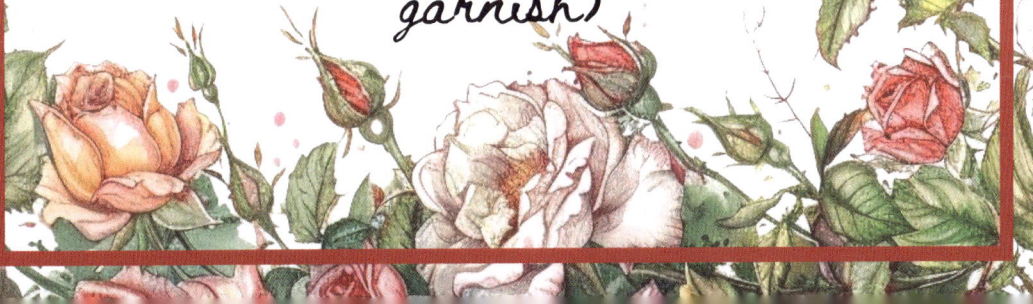

Instructions:

In a small saucepan, bring 2 cups of water to a gentle simmer over medium heat.

Once the water is simmering, add the dried rose petals to the saucepan.

If using fresh rose petals, ensure they are thoroughly washed and remove the white base of the petals before adding them to the water.

Allow the rose petals to steep in the simmering water for about 5-7 minutes, or until the water has taken on a light pink color and has a fragrant floral aroma.

After steeping, add the loose-leaf black tea to the saucepan. Let the tea steep for an additional 3-5 minutes, depending on your desired strength.

Once the tea has reached your desired strength, remove the saucepan from the heat and strain the rose-infused tea into cups using a fine mesh strainer or tea infuser.

If desired, sweeten the tea with honey or sugar to taste. Stir until the sweetener is fully dissolved.

Garnish each cup of tea with a fresh lemon slice for an extra burst of flavor and a touch of brightness.

Serve the rose-infused tea hot and enjoy its delicate floral aroma and soothing taste.

This fragrant and aromatic rose-infused tea is perfect for sipping on a cozy afternoon or for enjoying as a calming bedtime beverage.

Rose Infused Honey

Ingredients:

1 cup honey (raw and unpasteurized honey works best)

2-3 tablespoons dried rose petals (or 4-5 fresh rose petals)

Instructions:

Start by thoroughly washing the rose petals if using fresh ones. Ensure they are completely dry before proceeding. In a clean glass jar with a tight-fitting lid, place the dried rose petals or fresh rose petals.

Pour the honey over the rose petals in the jar, ensuring that they are fully submerged. Use a clean spoon to gently push down any petals that float to the top.

Seal the jar tightly with the lid and give it a gentle shake to ensure the rose petals are evenly distributed throughout the honey.

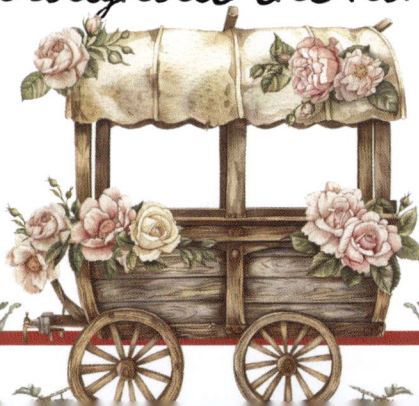

Place the jar in a cool, dark place to infuse for at least 1 week. The longer you let the honey infuse, the stronger the rose flavor will be.

Some people prefer to infuse their honey for up to 2-3 weeks for a more pronounced rose flavor.

My Recipes

Recipe:

_____

Ingredients

_____
_____
_____
_____
_____
_____
_____
_____
_____
_____
_____
_____

Directions

Recipe:

Ingredients

Directions

Recipe:

Ingredients

Directions

Recipe:

Ingredients

Directions

_____

_____

_____

_____

_____

_____

_____

_____

_____

_____

_____

_____

Recipe:

Ingredients

Directions

Recipe:

Ingredients

Directions

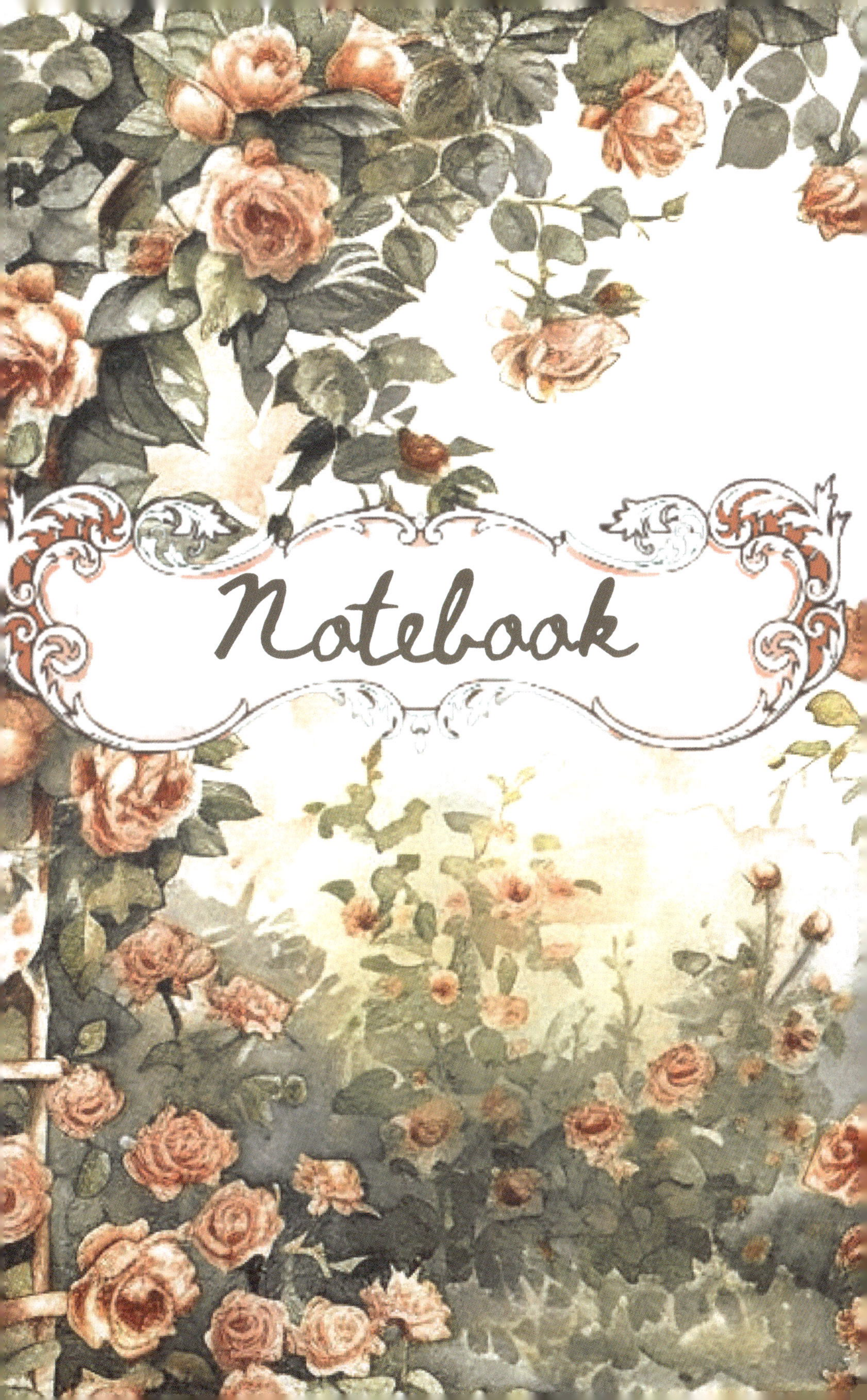
Notebook

Dear Friend,

As the final pages of this rose-themed cookbook journal turn, let them serve as a reminder of the enduring beauty and versatility of the rose.

From delicate petals adorning decadent desserts to fragrant infusions enhancing savory dishes, the rose has woven its way into the tapestry of culinary delights. May these recipes and reflections inspire you to infuse your own kitchen creations with the timeless elegance and enchanting aroma of this beloved flower.

As you embark on your culinary journey, may you savor each moment, delighting in the simple pleasures and exquisite flavors that the rose has to offer.

All my Love!

Verity Rose

Printed in Great Britain
by Amazon

47410290R00048